Again and Again
God Answers Prayer

MILTONETTA ATWATER

WESTBOW
PRESS®
A DIVISION OF THOMAS NELSON
& ZONDERVAN

This book is a work of non-fiction. Unless otherwise noted, the author
and the publisher make no explicit guarantees as to the accuracy of
the information contained in this book and in some cases, names of
people and places have been altered to protect their privacy.

Scripture quotations marked (NIV) are taken from the Holy Bible, New
International Version®, NIV®. Copyright © 1973, 1978, 1984, 2011 by Biblica,
Inc.™ Used by permission of Zondervan. All rights reserved worldwide. www.
zondervan.com The "NIV" and "New International Version" are trademarks
registered in the United States Patent and Trademark Office by Biblica, Inc.™

Scripture taken from the King James Version of the Bible.

WestBow Press books may be ordered through booksellers or by contacting:

WestBow Press
A Division of Thomas Nelson & Zondervan
1663 Liberty Drive
Bloomington, IN 47403
www.westbowpress.com
1 (866) 928-1240

Because of the dynamic nature of the Internet, any web addresses or
links contained in this book may have changed since publication and
may no longer be valid. The views expressed in this work are solely those
of the author and do not necessarily reflect the views of the publisher,
and the publisher hereby disclaims any responsibility for them.

Any people depicted in stock imagery provided by Getty Images are
models, and such images are being used for illustrative purposes only.
Certain stock imagery © Getty Images.

ISBN: 978-1-9736-2499-8 (sc)
ISBN: 978-1-9736-2500-1 (e)

Library of Congress Control Number: 2018904176

Print information available on the last page.

WestBow Press rev. date: 04/25/2018

INTRODUCTION

I learned after becoming a Child of God that I could have it all through Christ Jesus who saved me one day so many years ago. I never thought that my life would amount to what it is today. Because of Jesus Christ, who took my place at Calvary one day and bore all my sins and paid the ultimate price for me, I stand before a loving God whose Grace, Mercy and Righteousness is overwhelming. Without Him I would be nothing. Without Him, my life would not be worth living nor would I have the joy that captivates my heart each time my heavenly Father answers prayers.

On October 15, 2016, I lost my eldest son. Never could I have gone through such a devastating time in my life if I did not know a God that could answer prayer and take a situation so overwhelming and unexpected and turn it into a journey in my life that would sooth the very core of my heart; with an understanding in my spirit of His love for me while answering every prayer that I spoke out of my mouth and every prayer deeply hidden. I, at first, thought the journey was for my son but God showed me later that the journey was for me as He prepared me for the ultimate trust in Him of answers to my deepest prayers..........

"Because he loves me, " says the Lord,
"I will rescue him; I will protect him, for he
acknowledges my name. He will call upon me,
and I will answer him..........
Psalm 91:14 (NIV)

ACKNOWLEDGMENTS

I am indebted and so thankful to the Almighty God, Jesus Christ and HOLY SPIRIT in helping me to put this book together. Without being led, this book would have not been completed.

I thank my family, especially my siblings, Ladye, Dena (deceased), Victoria, Charles, Marilyn, Matthew and Pamela for their support at vital times in my life. I thank my sons Leslie, Jr. and Darryl who are the sunshine in my life.

I am grateful for my best friend of 38 years, Evangelist Connie Clark, who has been tremendously supportive and allowed me to use her as a sounding board.

I also want to express my sincere thanks to my good friends Dr. Beverly Swanson-Powell, Betty Gardner and Lynnis Woods-Mullins for their never ending encouragement in inspiring me in my endeavors.

Lastly, but certainly not the least, my pastors, Drs. Phillip G. and Brenda K. Goudeaux of Calvary Christian Center in Sacramento, California for loving the Lord with all their might and teaching the gospel so that I could stand before the Lord and realize the plans and purposes that He has for my life.

PRELUDE

It was early in the morning and the sun was coming up.

"Oh no," my mom moaned, "we are out of milk again. Gotta get to the store before everyone wakes up."

I was nine months old at that time and just as cute as a butterball I was told. My mother always got up early to make sure that the house was warm and that all would be well before everyone started moving around for she loved talking to the Lord early in the morning and her prayer was always; Lord, take care of my family as the day rolls on. My mother believed in talking to the Lord about everything. She would pray in the morning, in the evening and right before we all went to bed. My dad felt that talking to the Lord on a daily basis was a waste of time because if he needed God to do something he would talk to him then. Being the first born in the family made my birth something special. My aunts and uncles would come by and say "where is that special bundle of joy that you prayed for?" You see, before I was born, my mother prayed for a baby because it seemed like she would never get pregnant. But God had mercy on my mother and I was born, so to my mom, I was an answer to prayer. My dad wanted a son but I think he was satisfied that God gave him a girl. My mom always cradled me like I was special and would lay her hands on my head as she thanked God each day for my delivery. Each night before I would be put down to sleep she would make sure that I was tucked in real good. The sheets were tucked in and around the bed so tightly that a bug couldn't even crawl through. That was my mother's way of making sure I didn't fall out of the bed at night. Because I was such a fretful child, I would wiggle my way to the bottom of the bed at times and when my mother came in some mornings to get me, she would be terrified because I would be at the very bottom of the bed and couldn't move. The first time she found me like that, she was beside herself. She would pray, "Lord, take care of my baby and keep her safe." She just couldn't understand why I just wouldn't be still and remain at the top of the bed and not hidden under the covers.

Mom left everyone asleep and figured she would get back before anyone woke up. But I woke up and tried to wiggle my way out of the bed. Because the sheets were so tight around my neck and because my bed was high up from the floor, trying to get out of the bed was quite a trick. I found myself dangling from the side of the bed and not quite sure what to do. I guess I was waiting for my mom or dad to come and get me because I didn't move a muscle. My mother walked into the room and saw me dangling on the side of the bed. She ran to my side and couldn't believe how I had become entangled in the sheets and was wedged between the wall and the bed with eyes wide awake just waiting for someone to come to the rescue. My mother let out a scream and woke the entire house up and although I was startled I didn't move. My mother told me later that if I had moved an inch I would have choked myself to death as the sheet was secured around my neck very tightly and I was hanging from the bed in a noose. You see, my mother prayed for me, and God answered her prayers for my safety. That moment begin a battle that I didn't quite understand until I started walking with the Lord. The devil wanted to take my life but God had a plan and purpose and thus begins the journey as God answers prayer...........

ONE

The beginning

I was 24 yrs. old, fresh out of college and ready to embark on a career in business. Many of my friends had gotten married while in college but I had aspirations and goals and the thought of becoming a wife and mother at my age had not even entered my mind until I met a real nice guy who made a great impression on me. I couldn't believe that he was paying attention to me. I didn't date much while in college so I couldn't really compare him to many of the men that I considered just friends. He was already in his career and was looking for a wife. He spoke gently to me and shared his dreams and aspirations. He planned our lives together and didn't leave much room for me to even think that my life could be any other way but with him and the way he planned everything. I said yes to his proposal and we got married and started a family right away. I was very happy. My dear husband wanted me to stay home and care for our family as he promised to take care of us and make sure that we wanted for nothing.

We were married for fourteen years and had three wonderful daughters. My life was like a whirlwind, exciting and eventful and at times very challenging as being a full time mother kept me very busy. My parents came to see me often and would remark that I wasn't in church and serving the Lord. In my own way, I loved the Lord but life just seemed so busy and everything was going so well.

1

Dave joined a new firm and soon was made a partner and I was making sure that everything at home was functioning well so that when Dave came home, he would have no complaints. I wanted to be the best wife and mother I could possibly be. But my mother reminded me that God should be first in everything that I do. I felt that God was first and really didn't understand her insistence in me reading the word of God every day. As far as I was concerned things were going just fine.

The girls were really growing up and becoming more involved in drama classes, music and sports. I even considered going back to school myself since it seemed like the girls didn't need much of my time and attention any longer but I thought about it and decided that they needed me more. My job was at home and that's the way Dave and I wanted it.

Then one day, Dave informed me that he was taking a job four hundred miles away and that it would be better if we did not relocate with him. I couldn't quite understand why he would accept a position so far away but Dave wanted the best for us and if taking a position that was distant would be worthy of future promotions, that is what he felt he should do. I was glad for him that he was climbing the ladder of success but also mindful of the fact that the girls needed him also. Our relationship wasn't as close as it was when we first got married and I sensed a growing apart and at first it bothered me but I didn't quite know what to do other than to be the best wife that I could be and a good mother to our girls.

I called my mom and dad and told them the news. I called the girls together and explained that things were going to be a bit different around the house now and that their Dad would no longer be living with us during the week. They couldn't quite understand what was happening because they had been so sheltered from the real pain of fear, disappointments and the stresses of this world. Change of this sort was new for them. I couldn't even remember the last time I had taken the girls to church or even spoken to them about God. Now I needed God to help me and I didn't even know where to begin. I tried to talk to God before going to bed but I felt so ashamed to approach him because I didn't know what to say. Should I reintroduce myself to him again, would he even remember who I was.....after all I went to Sunday school and attended church with my parents.

I didn't even know where to begin or even what to say but I knew that the Lord my mother talked about so often would somehow help me in my distress. I knew I had to find my way back to where it all began.

I searched for a church in my neighborhood. I found out that one of my old friends from high school went to a church not too far from my house, so I attended there with the girls that Sunday. It wasn't quite what I was looking for but I still attended so that my heart would be content knowing that I was at least headed in the right direction. Laura, my middle daughter, asked me one Sunday, "how do I get saved"? I told her that we were going to church now and that we are Christians because we are in church. Somehow in my mind that didn't quite sound right so I began to again question my relationship with God. I called my girlfriend who had invited us to church that Sunday and I ask her what does one have to do to be saved. She explained to me that I had to repent of my sins, surrender my life to the Lord and ask Him to come into my heart. She gave me some scriptures to read, specifically:

That if thou shalt confess with thy mouth the Lord Jesus, and shalt believe in thine heart that God raised him from the dead, thou shalt be saved. For with the heart man believeth unto righteousness; and with the mouth confession is made unto salvation. (Romans 10:9,10 KJV)

I went home and read those scriptures. It was almost frightening to realize that I didn't know that I needed to be saved by accepting Jesus Christ as my Lord and savior and confessing my sins. I couldn't believe that I had allowed myself to be in the dark for so long. It was as though I was hearing what my mother was saying all those years about getting back in church and putting God first in my life. I thought I was alright with God because I didn't do drugs, I didn't cheat on my husband, I hadn't committed a murder, none of those things that I thought would send me to a place called hell. I couldn't believe that I had been missing the mark all of those years. Yet, I could feel that God still loved me because as I knelt down on my knees and cried out to him, I could sense his tender love for me. I became aware of his warmth comforting me. I knew I couldn't wait to go to church that Sunday; I had to ask God into my life right then. I knelt before God and made him my Lord and Savior that night on my knees in my bedroom. God and I talked awhile and I knew my journey was beginning because now I had become a born-again Christian and again God answered prayer......

TWO

Supplied Needs

I found a job as a Administrative Assistant in a small office not too far from my home. It was perfect because I could be home before the girls arrived and could have dinner ready for them. Dave was up for the weekend and came by to have me sign some papers regarding the house and noticed something different about me.

"Wow, you seem happy. What's going on with you?"

"I am a born-again Christian now, and that makes me really happy. Have you ever thought about making Jesus your Lord and Savior, Dave?"

"No, actually, I haven't thought about it and quite frankly, I don't see the need for some book telling me what I can do and what I can't do. I don't need a crutch to lean on; I am doing quite well by myself. Don't try and hogwash our girls Megan and turn their lives into nun hood. I want them to be normal and have fun growing up and doing things that they like."

"Dave, I want the same thing for our girls too but I want them to also know the Lord so that they can make good and wise decisions as they grow up."

"I am not going to argue with you about this Megan, gotta go and catch up on some work. Tell the girls I couldn't stay but I will see them next weekend."

I didn't tell Dave that I needed help with support for the girls and his being so far away and the expenses it was causing was draining our account. I wanted to be able to take care of them without his help and I guess pride kind of got in the way too. I looked at our checkbook and realized that I was down to our last dime and really didn't have enough to buy groceries. I sat on the bed and began to wonder. "What am I going to do Lord?" I don't want to bother my parents because they have helped me so much already. I don't want to ask Dave because I want him to see that I don't need his help and that I can make it without him.

"Lord, you have got to help me". I picked up the bible and just flipped through some pages when I came across a highlighted scripture that said:

But my God shall supply all your need according to his riches and glory by Christ Jesus. (Phil 4:19 KJV)

I looked at that and told the Lord that if this was true, I needed him to show up quickly because I had gotten really low on food to feed my children. The door bell rang and my friend from down the street was at the door. She asked me if I wanted to attend a prayer meeting with her that night. I told her that I was just about to get ready for dinner. She said not to worry about cooking tonight because at the church where the prayer meeting was taking place, they were serving dinner that evening. So I went to the prayer meeting with her. I told the girls that I was going out for a while and to do their homework and that we would eat when I returned.

At the prayer meeting, there was a visiting Evangelist. I didn't know very much about evangelism and wasn't sure about some things that I saw going on in this meeting. I had heard about people being filled with the Holy Spirit and speaking in tongues but I didn't really know too much about this. I was very curious but I didn't want to try anything that was not of God. You see, I had told God that I wanted to be the best Christian that I could be and that I wanted to do all things right in his sight. If he said don't wear makeup, I would stop wearing makeup. If he said don't wear pants I would stop wearing pants. I didn't want to do anything that would make God displeased with me. I didn't understand a lot about the Bible but I knew that God was a good God and I could sense His presence in my life and I knew that he was real. Things just seemed so different and I wanted to do all that I could to please the Lord.

The evangelist that was speaking ask me to come to the front of the church as she had done with several other people. She said a word over them and said some things to them that made some lift their hands or fall to the floor. I had already told the Lord that if this is not of God, I was not going to fall down. I had never believed in playing with God and I wasn't going to be tricked either. The lady smiled at me and gently touched my forehead. She told me that God had a special plan and purpose for my life and that it was going to be a long and slow process but that I would one day be truly happy. That touched my spirit and before I knew it I had fallen to the floor. When I got up I wasn't sure what had taken place but I knew that this was real because I sensed a knowing in my spirit that this was of God. As we were getting ready to leave, I got into my girlfriends car and she had gathered together three bags of groceries for me. My mouth dropped and I asked her how she knew that I needed some food. She simply smiled and said, "God is good and greatly to be praised." I couldn't believe that God cared that much about me that he would nudge someone that I hadn't seen in years and prompt them to do this for me.

And again, God answered prayer in a way that I never thought he would. He took a heart that was devoted to him and obeyed him to meet my need. What a mighty God we serve……..

THREE

Baptized in the Spirit

I was dropping the girls off at school and noticed that the gas was getting pretty low. Even though my office wasn't that far from home I still had a little distance to take the girls to school because I wanted them to finish the year out at their old school before transferring into our current district. I again thought of calling Dave about our needs but my pride just wouldn't let me. I got in the car and made my way to the kid's school to drop them off. I had to take the freeway and I just don't know what I was thinking but I was in the fast lane when the car started slowing down and I knew instantly that I had run out of gas. I told the girls to sit quietly. I didn't know what I was going to do. The cars were passing by and I was becoming scared. My heart began to beat real hard not really knowing what I was going to do. I whispered, "Oh Lord, please help me." All of a sudden, a truck pulled up behind my car. I couldn't see the person very well but I did see a gas can. I wondered to myself. How did he know that I had run out of gas? So many things were going on in my mind. How could I pay him for the gas, what was I going to do if he tried something. Before I knew it, he had popped the hood of the car. I told the girls to be very quiet and that I was going to get out and talk to the man that was putting gas in the car. When I got the courage to get out of the car, I didn't see the person who had popped the hood. It was only a matter of a few minutes and I couldn't believe that this person who had stopped to rescue me was no longer in sight. I looked around and there was no truck and no body visible to the eye. I couldn't believe what had just happened. My car had gas in it and I didn't see who put it in nor was I able to thank this someone who had supplied my need. Oh my, I couldn't believe this. I started the car and drove home. Tears started flowing because I knew God was in this thing that had just happened. I remember thinking to myself that God's word said that He would supply all of my needs. I remembered while sitting in church several Sundays before, that one of the mothers of the church told me that God was truly going to bless me. I was going through such a hard time but somehow I knew that I was not alone. I knew that God was with me. Didn't know how God was going to bless me but somehow I begin to see that I could depend on him. I begin to go to a bible study every week at the home of one of the ladies in my neighborhood. I begin to see that being a Christian somehow put you in contact with other Christians. I didn't understand a lot about the word but I was seeking the Lord. I would pray and ask God to give me wisdom because I just couldn't seem to understand a lot of what I thought some of the ladies seem to grasp right away. They would be talking about the word and it seemed so complicated and over my head. I felt a lot of times that they were talking above my level of understanding. I would kneel before the Lord many times and ask him to help me understand in simple terms the things he was saying in the bible. I almost became discouraged because I couldn't talk with them. Then one evening, one of the ladies ask me if I wanted to receive the baptism of the Holy Spirit. I was somewhat reluctant because I didn't know if this was real or not but I told her that I want all that God has for me and if this is real then I want it. I had resigned myself to the fact that I was not going to fabricate some made up language and that if this was really of God then he was going to have to do it. We went into a back room where she read some scriptures to me.

And I say unto you, Ask, and it shall be given to you; seek, and ye shall find; knock, and it shall be opened unto you. For

***every one that asketh receiveth; and to him that knocketh it shall
be opened.*** (Luke 11: 9,10 KJV)

I humbled myself before the Lord and told him that this is in
his hands and that I just wanted what he wanted for me. The lady
laid her hands on my head and began to pray. All of a sudden, I felt
this quiver on my lips and a leaping in my spirit that was no mistake
because out of my mouth an utterance began. I was speaking in
an unknown tongue and the more I spoke the better I felt. I knew
it was God because I could not have done this on my own. I kept
going on and on and I didn't want to stop because I felt as if I was
praising God in this unknown tongue. I was so happy to have gone
through this experience. After receiving the baptism of the Holy
Spirit I seem to understand the scriptures a lot better. It seemed like
the word started jumping out at me and a revelation that I never
knew existed was there. I was so happy to receive the baptism of the
Holy Spirit because I now realized a connection with the Lord that
I relished beyond comprehension. There was a power I began to feel
when I prayed. I was growing to understand the word much better
and I liked it. And again, God answered prayer for I began to walk
in a direction of more understanding in my walk with Christ........

As I began to continue to go to Bible Study and read the word
it seemed like so many things begin to happen. I was so excited
about the things that were happening in my life. I had found a good
church and my Christian friends really were kind and helpful to me.
I began to search for more of God and wanted to know more about
the things in the spirit and the prophetic things of God. I found
myself attending a Church of God in Christ where an evangelist was
calling certain people up to the front of the church and prophesying
different things about them. I wasn't really sure what to expect
because a lady did tell me some things that I had been wondering
about and God used her to answer some questions that I had. And
because of this I wanted to know more about the things he had in
store for me and to give me more direction. I found myself going
to different churches searching for someone to tell me something

about the things happening in my life. A little lady laid hands on me and I literally fell to the floor without her barely touching me. I couldn't understand the meaning of what she was doing but I just wanted God to talk to me and tell me things because it seemed like I was still going through such a rough time. I wanted to know that everything was going to be alright. I wanted him to tell me that Dave was going to become a Christian and that everything was going to be just like it was but even better now because we would both be Christians. I was searching and looking for answers. I didn't realize that the long and slow process was beginning and God's timing was not my timing and that as I read the word of God the Holy Spirit would lead and guide my footsteps and anchor me along the way.

FOUR

Angels appear

I was folding clothes the next day when my oldest daughter stated that she saw an angel. I didn't really pay too much attention to what she was saying because I hadn't really considered whether I really believed her or not. I know that kids can have vivid imaginations and I didn't want hers to extend too far. So I didn't make too much of it. Then my youngest daughter stated that she saw an angel in my bedroom. Well, I started to take notice then because my youngest wasn't prone to much imagination as my oldest. I asked her what the angel was doing and she stated that the angel was standing with her wings raised up like she was looking up at the sky. And then she stated that she saw angels sitting by everyone in her classroom. I was amazed at this and wondered what was going on. Could God really be allowing my girls to see angels. Could this really be happening? I wondered about this even more because I didn't know what to expect next. Would I start seeing angels too…. What was God trying to do? I wasn't afraid, I just did not understand the purpose for this happening. We were driving to the store one afternoon and I asked the girls if they saw the angels and they both said that the angels were flying on both sides of the car. I was totally amazed but not quite convinced. We were stopped behind a car and I saw a symbol on the back of a car that looked strange. All of a sudden, the symbol changed when I looked closer at it and it said "Jesus is the answer". I couldn't believe what I was seeing and I asked my girls to look and tell me what they saw, and they said the same thing "Jesus is the answer". When I looked at the symbol again as the car was beginning to move, the symbol changed back to what it originally looked like. I wondered to myself why these things were happening to me. Was God trying to let me know that I was not alone. Was he letting me know that wherever I go he is right there with me always. I remembered reading about Joshua and how God told him that he would never leave him nor forsake him…..was God trying to tell me the same thing. When we got back home, my youngest daughter told me that an angel was with me. She said that the angel was by my side but much taller than I was and that she didn't look like me but had curly hair. I said, "do you think you can talk to the angel and ask the angel a question for me"? I wanted to get to the bottom of this and at the same time, my curiosity was getting the better of me too. I said to my oldest daughter, "ask the angel if I will ever sing in a church choir". You see I had never sung in a church choir but I always desired to do this when listening to different church choirs. The songs would stir up my heart and minister to my spirit. My daughter answered, "the angel said that it will not be you singing but the spirit within you." Tears came to my eyes as I knew beyond the shadow of a doubt that these angels were being seen and heard by my girls. Because of her age and lack of knowledge of the word, I knew that she was not old enough to say such words to me and that God was using them to let me know that my kids were being watched over by him as I prayed each day for them and that he was with me always. I kept crying as I begin to truly realize that God loved me so much that he would do this for me. He was hearing my prayers and knew my heart and loved me enough to go beyond just a regular way of doing things and touch me in a special way. I no longer needed to know if what was happening was real or not for I knew it was real. I never saw any angels nor needed to see to believe. I didn't ask my children any more questions. I just knew that whatever happened next God was in it and taking care of me.

Dave called and wanted to spend some time with the girls. He hadn't done that in a while and that really made me glad. He was spending so much time at work that I wondered if he even cared about their welfare or wondered if their needs were being met. I guess that as long as I said nothing, he felt that things were alright. I loved my girls and wanted the best for them and somehow I knew that they needed the love and attention of their father as well as my love for them. Dave arrived around 6:00 pm and wanted to take them out for dinner. They were so happy to see him and just gave him no room for air as they hugged and tussled with their dad. I felt so good seeing them together and wondered to myself, how did things go so wrong. What could I have done differently?

"Well Dave, you know they have school tomorrow, so please don't have them out too late."

"Megan, don't tell me how to take care of my children. I know when to bring them back."

I froze because I didn't want to turn this into an ordeal. I didn't like walking on egg shells like before so I didn't say anything else. The less said, the better the tension in the atmosphere. Why do I have to make all the adjustments whenever he came around, I ask myself. Why do I always have to keep the peace? Well, I thought to myself. Someone has to be the adult. That's the excuse I gave myself and that's the excuse that made me feel better. Thoughts of when Dave and I were together lingered in my mind. Even though Dave had not settled down in his new place yet, it continually seemed like we were so far apart and my hopes of being a family again tore at my heart. I desperately wanted to salvage our marriage but so much had taken place. He accepted a job for away and a different life. How could I change when I had no idea what he wanted in a wife. Dave never could really tell me why he felt the need to be so far away from us other than to secure and make more money for materialist comfort. My whole world was centered around Dave and our children. I had no life other than being a wife and mother. I thought back on when I was in school and yearning to have a career of my own. Where did those dreams go? How could I have let a mere human being detract me from being a successful woman in a career? How did I shortchange myself into believing that I could not be what I set out to be because I became a mother and wife? It wasn't Dave's fault and I knew that I had to somehow get my life back together. I ask Dave about the job promotion and when he would be making changes in his living arrangements and he mumbled something about putting it on hold.

"What do you mean you put it on hold?" "Are you saying that you want to work on our marriage?"

"No, I didn't say that."

"Well, what are you saying?"

"I just need some time to sort a few things out, Megan. Give me a break, ok, I just need time to think. Things have been so hectic and I need some space."

I didn't know what to think about this. Part of my heart was hopeful because I had prayed so hard for my marriage to work, more so for my children. I wanted them to have the safe and secure feeling of having a mother and a father with them each day to protect them and give them the love they so deserved. I didn't know what I was feeling these days about Dave because so many things had changed. I was beginning to realize that God had a special plan and purpose for me. I didn't quite know what it was but I knew that I didn't want to go back into the same kind of relationship that I had with Dave. I wanted more and I knew that I deserved more.

"Dave, at some point we do need to talk. I can't and I won't put my life on hold for you to be comfortable in your space. I need to know what is going on."

"Megan, I don't know what is going on. I don't know what to say. I do know that I am not going to holy roll with you in this new found religion that you say you have found. Every time your mother comes to visit that's all she talks about. God this and God that. I am not going to put up with this. I don't need this."

Part of me wanted to say you don't have to put up with it and part of me wanted to give him what he wanted. I was so confused and needed God to tell me what to do. I just stood there and didn't say anything else to Dave because my fear of what was happening took over me. I wanted things to be as they were but yet I had found a peace that I wasn't sure I wanted to relinquish.

"Okay Dave, I will wait for your answer."

Was God testing me? Did he want to see if I really wanted my marriage to work. I just wasn't sure of what to think at this time. I wasn't even sure of how I was supposed to pray now. I just wanted God to change Dave and make him the father and husband that I wanted him to be. Dave finally left with the girls and I started to cry.

"What am I going to do Lord?"

I dropped to my knees in my bedroom and I began to talk to God again. I found so much solace on bended knee and it seemed like I could feel his arms so softly surrounding me letting me know that everything was going to be alright. I began to cry because I just didn't know if I could take this anymore.

"When is this going to be over Lord, I cried out."

In the stillness of my bedroom, God comforted me and in my spirit I heard Him say, be still and know that I am God. I felt so much love and peace surround my bedroom and I became so overwhelmed with excited love for God that he would love me that much to take the time to comfort and talk to me. I wanted more and more of what I was understanding in my spirit because in him I felt safety and that with him I knew that nothing could go wrong. I didn't realize how long I had been on my knees talking to the Lord. I stood up and began to get ready for bed. The girls had already returned so I just looked in on them to make sure that all was well and then went back to my bedroom. As I walked down the hallway to my bedroom I begin to fear the dark as never before. I had such a fear of the dark. Now that I was beginning to have a sense of security with the Lord, I didn't like this fear that still remained in my life. I remembered a scripture that I had read in the bible about fear. I called my friend and ask her to give me that scripture so that I could look it up again. II Timothy 1:7 was the scripture. I opened my bible and I spoke that word repeatedly aloud to myself.

For God has not given us a spirit of fear; but of power, and of love, and of a sound mind. (II Timothy 1: 7 KJV)

I kept saying those words to myself over and over again and each night as I walked down the hallway to my bedroom I began to believe what I was saying. I was beginning to have no fear walking down the hallway. I was so amazed because I was not afraid anymore. I couldn't believe what was happening. I had lived with so much fear of the dark for so long that I didn't even think I could live any other way. Much to my amazement I was learning that God was doing a good work in me. I smiled with joy and amazement over the things that God was doing. Each time I read his word I could feel his love radiate throughout my entire being. I begin to learn so much about this God that my mother seemed to love and adore so much. Yes, I knew that I had found something different than I thought I was going to find and my heart was so glad. Yes, God had again answered prayer and was becoming a might in my life that I was learning to lean and depend upon..........

Dave began to spend more time with us and although I was going to church each Sunday and beginning to walk with the Lord with new confidence in his word, I thought things were going to be different. Dave came and went as he pleased. He hadn't changed at all and I was terrified that I had let my freedom in having peace in my household no longer be. What had I done? The girls were ecstatic about having their father around all the time. They didn't seem to feel the same emptiness that I felt. They yearned to have his presence even if it was only for a little while in the evenings. They loved their father so much and wanted him in the home with us. I settled because I thought it would get better but it got worse. I walked on egg shells most of the time because it seemed like I could never do anything right. If a check bounced because there was no money in the account, it was always my fault. If something happened at school with one of the girls, it seemed to always be my fault that it happened. I could never seem to do anything right. I felt as though I was cornered in a situation that I couldn't get out of and I wondered to God, why is this happening.? I thought life was going to be a bed of roses because I had given my life to him. I couldn't believe the transition that had taken place. Where did my peace go? I resigned myself to just go with the flow. I had a job that I liked and new friends and although my walk with the Lord had grown I began to become very content with some things. I joined another church and threw myself into work in the ministry. I took the girls with me whenever I went to church and that seemed to please Dave but he never went with us to any of the services. Many people knew that I was married and just like many of the other married women in the church we came by ourselves.

I told Dave that my car seemed like it needed some work done on it. The radiator was overheating and I wasn't sure if it was going to stop at some point. I was driving home one evening when I saw the red light come on and an indication that the radiator was running hot. It was getting dark now because the time had changed. I begin to pray silently to myself that if the car stopped it would stop in a lite area where I could see. As God heard me, the car stopped right under a light at the corner. I got out of the car with my heels on and proceeded to walk to the nearest place where I could call home for help. As I was walking, I realized how dark it had gotten and because the word of God was in my spirit and I knew how to pray, I said " Lord, you have not given me a spirit of fear, but of power, love and a sound mind, I will not fear this dark." As I spoke those words, it seemed as though the entire area around me lit up. I smiled and begin to thank God for strong legs to walk with and knew that I was not walking by myself. As I continued to walk, this black truck passed and then slowed up in front of me. I thought to myself, this person is probably going to ask me if I need a ride. For some reason, I began to have an ill feeling about this because the windows were tinted dark on all sides and I couldn't make out who was in the truck. I begin to pray again. "Lord, you said you would always give me a way of escape, I am not going to get into that truck, you need to help me NOW". A second later another car drove up within seconds of me coming to this truck and two young ladies rolled down their windows and ask me if I wanted a ride. My heart was pounding so hard and yet my heart was made so glad because God was right on time. I said yes to the young ladies and got inside of the car. As I was riding with them, the passenger stated to me that as they were driving by earlier she saw me as they passed and told her friend that something told her that they needed to turn around and go back and pick me up. They turned around at the light and proceeded back my way and turned to be on the same side as I was walking. I shared with her how afraid I was because of the truck that was in front of us with its tinted windows. She commented on that too and stated they were glad they had come along when they did. They drove me all the way home. Because I knew that God was with me, I was so overwhelmed to see how much he cared that he would touch the hearts of two women that didn't even know me and have them rescue me. What a mighty God we serve.......and again God answers prayer in a way that signified His unmerited love for me.

FIVE

Depending on the Word

I began to become absorbed in my work not really thinking about my marriage other than praying every day that things would be alright and that the peace that I so desperately wanted would be at home when I returned each day. But I dreaded going home and I just could not seem to understand what was happening. Why was I going through so much turmoil? Why was I afraid all of the time except when I was at work? I sought the Lord for answers to these questions. I went to Bible Study each week and tried to remember as many scriptures as I could. I enjoyed studying the word of God and would read to my girls the different stories in the bible of biblical times and to be honest I think I got more out of telling the stories than they did just listening to me. I just wanted so much to understand who God really was and just what he wanted from us as his people. Why did so many people seem to suffer in wanting to do what the bible says we should do? I talked to God in the mornings before I would go to work. On bended knee I would cry out to Him and tell him about the things I was going through and how much I loved him because of the things he was doing for me and my girls but the gnawing concern that I was having was always the same. Why so much pain and heartache? Then I begin to realize some things in my life. God didn't make me take Dave back into our lives. I made a conscious decision to allow him to come back into our lives. God was not going to make Dave love me the way it says that a man should love and treat his wife but his word was available to Dave just like it was available to me. God helped me to understand that choice is given to each of us to accept or reject his word. God helped me understand that it all about the choices and decisions we make in our lives and the only thing that I am responsible for is making my decisions and being the wife that the Lord had called me to be. I could possibly win over Dave through living the word but it was still his choice.

Then I began the journey of reading as many books as I could on how to be a good wife and mother. I wanted so much to please my husband that I became anesthetized to his faults. I made excuses and looked the other way. Our girls needed their father's attention but his work came first. We again started arguing over little things which turned into big issues. We were so at odds with one another that the comfort that I treasured in having a secure and wonderful life with the man that I thought I would spend the rest of my life with became only a dream once again. I wanted so much for him to realize that he had a wife that loved and cared for him and wanted his soul one day to be in saved. I just couldn't seem to understand why I put myself though this. The girls began to notice how things had changed and had feelings of being uneasy and that bothered me greatly. I could go through this but I didn't want my girls to suffer when I didn't feel that this was their battle. My prayers began to change. I wanted Dave to leave our home so that we could have peace. I told the Lord that his word says that He would never give us any more than we could bear and that's what I needed at this time and I needed things to change for the better. I couldn't confront Dave because I wasn't sure how he would react. I began to learn that the battle in spiritual matters were not mine but belonged to God so I prayed for a change and God was true to his word. Dave received another promotion. He was so excited and wanted to leave right away to start his new position. I was genuinely happy for him also because I knew that he worked very hard at his job and deserved his promotion. He seemed to always put his best foot forward when it came to his job. He wanted the best for his girls and never fretted on giving them the things that they wanted or needed. He provided for us generously. There were times when he seemed to actually want to be different from the way that he was but another part of him seemed to take first place and it was a battle within himself that he chose not to fight and tried to ignore most of the time as it appeared to me. I looked at Dave and wondered where did the man that I met in school and married go. He had changed so much or was it that I really didn't know the man that I married.

Dave packed his clothes and kissed the girls good-bye. He explained to them that he was going to be gone during the week but that he would return on the weekends because his job took him too for away to be home each day. They cried and tried to understand but Kimmy was daddy's girl and she yearned to be more of a part of his life and couldn't quite understand why he would leave us again. She didn't like the tension that it caused when he was here but she didn't want him away from her either. Kimmy ran to her room and would not come out for dinner. I left her alone for a while because she needed time to herself to absorb what was happening. She hurt as I did when Dave first left and as I began to adjust Kimmy didn't adjust as well. She had nightmares and stomachaches that just wouldn't seem to go away. I prayed for Kimmy and loved her with a force so great because I didn't want to see her hurt. I could go through the fire of a battle with life but I didn't want her to have to go through this being so young as she could not understand the problems that we were having and the fact that we couldn't be with him as before. I just wanted this pain and frustration of life to go away. I didn't realize that sometimes when we go through the fire and trials of life, we are growing up and maturing in the word of God and learning how to walk and lean more on God. I prayed for my girls fervently and continuously and as they began to ease into the new situation of their father again being gone during the week and only home on the weekends, things began to settle into a routine.

"Mom, I want to join the school choir, can I please, please," begged Kimmy. We practice twice a week after school and my grades are good," said Kimmy.

"Let me think about it, Kimmy, you know that sometimes I have to work late and I want to make sure you have a way to get home after practice."

"Mom, I can ride with Steve. His dad just bought him a new car and he said that he would bring me home after practice."

"Kimmy, you have been spending a lot of time with Steve lately and I am not sure how I feel about this. He seems like a nice boy but I just don't want you to depend on him bringing you home after practice. Since when did you start liking school choir?"

"Mom, I sing in the choir at church, so why wouldn't I like singing in the choir at school?"

"Well, it seems like I have to always push you to go choir rehearsal at church and you just didn't seem to have that much interest before so I was just wondering what changed your mind about singing now?"

"I don't know Mom, lately when I sing, I just feel so different. It seems like I feel so good singing for the Lord and I don't want it to ever end. I shared it with Steve and he is the one who suggested that I might want to join the school choir. Steve has become such a good friend and he is going through some things at home similar to what I am feeling at times. His father is always gone and we share a lot about how much we both miss our fathers."

"Oh, ok, I didn't know. I am glad though that you are finding a sense of wanting to enjoy the presence of the Lord through singing. What days and how long does practice go in the evenings? I want to know Steve's mother's name also."

"Mom, she goes to our church. You know Mrs. Anderson. That's Steve's Mom."

"No, I didn't know that. She's very nice. I have to make it a point to introduce myself the next time we are in church. She is awfully quite but really nice. Don't forget to tell Linda that you are not walking with her after school when you have school choir so that she can find someone else to walk with. I don't want her walking by herself".

Kimmy turned and walked out the door relieved that she was going to be able to join the school choir. Of course, she really wanted to join the choir but she also wanted to be with Steve. They were becoming very close friends and she liked the way she was feeling when she was with him. Things just seemed to be so good between them and she wanted to be with him every waking minute. He seemed to enjoy being with her too and she felt that they had become very good friends. Although she was only 15 and he was 16 they were becoming an item at school because they spent so much time together. They had never kissed or held hands but their conversations were so relaxing that she felt she could tell him any and everything.

"Steve, my mom said that I could join the school choir and get a ride with you after practice. I am so excited about being in the choir."

"Oh, ok Kimmy. Gloria will be joining us after practice too. She decided to join the choir and ask if she could get a ride home too. She lives right next door so she will be joining us. I didn't know she was even interested in singing. Wow, this is going to be great. Mrs. Carpenter was asking us to recruit people for the choir and it seems like we are getting quite a few people who are interested."

"I didn't know she was interested in singing either Steve."

"Yea, that's really weird. I have known Gloria a long time and she was always so tomboyish but she is really changing. She started wearing all this make-up and stuff and she kind of looks so grown now. Not sure what to think sometimes. So glad you don't put all of that stuff on your face. You look really nice without all that."

"Wow, thanks Steve, I didn't know that you even noticed how I look."

The school bell rung and it was time for first period. Steve, Gloria and Kimmy took English the first period together and now that Gloria was going to be in the school choir with both of them, things all of a sudden started to feel kind of funny. Kimmy kept looking at Gloria out of the side of her eye wondering just what kind of girl she was. She had known of Gloria but didn't really hang around her circle of friends. Yes, Gloria had started wearing make-up and she did look pretty good but she had never really considered her as a level of competition between her and Steve. Did Steve really seriously like her and just didn't say anything. Kimmy found herself secretly watching Steve and Gloria just to see how they acted toward one another. She caught Gloria smile at Steve and of course he smiled back. Kimmy felt a knife pierce her heart. Lord, what is going on here. Why am I feeling like this? Is this what they call being jealous. I don't like the thoughts that are running through my mind. This is insane. I have to get a grip on myself. After all, Steve and I are just friends. Do I really want to be that girl who comes unglued just because her friend starts liking someone else besides her? What do I say to Steve to let him know how I feel.

"Kimmy, what are you waiting on? Class is over. You better get to your next class before the bell rings. See you this evening. Don't forget choir is tonight."

"Ok, Steve, thanks. See you later."

Choir went pretty well and quite a few people joined. I was really surprised and tried not to think about the fact that Gloria was with us and seemed to really have a good voice. We headed toward Steve's car and before I realized what was happening, Gloria jumped in the front seat and I just stood there wondering what had just happened. Steve didn't say anything other than "hop in, let's go". My heart sank and I almost couldn't breathe. I tried to smile and joke as we proceeded home but I was boiling inside. I couldn't join in on the conversations because my whole body was reacting. I didn't know whether to punch Gloria in the back of her head or just be silent and let them enjoy their conversation by themselves. So many conflicting things were going on in my mind and it was almost like I was losing control of my thoughts. I imagined them being together after they let me out at my house and probably going someplace else to have fun without me.

"Kimmy, how do you like Mr. Stone, our first period teacher? Isn't he the bomb? I think he is so cute. Melanie said that he is not even married. I can't imagine a hunk of a man like him still single."

"Yea, he is good looking, I guess. I never really noticed."

"Kimmy, how could you not notice? The way he smiles is so awesome. Oh, this is where you live. Well, good night Kimmy, see you tomorrow in class."

"Good night, Kimmy. See you tomorrow in first period, said Steve".

His eyes did linger but she now couldn't determine if it was just friendship or a longing to be just with her like always and before. Kimmy went inside and just felt so lonely in what she was experiencing and going through. She couldn't talk to her mom because she had her own set of problems and didn't know if her mother would understand or just have a fit because her daughter was jealous and had this crush on a boy. Getting ready for bed had just become a chore. I tried to concentrate on washing my face and brushing my teeth but every time I attempted this I wanted to call Steve and find out if he was at home or not. I kept trying to think of so many excuses as to why I would call. Did I accidentally leave something in his car that evening? Did Mr. Stone give us some homework that I didn't quite understand and I needed Steve to help me with it? Would it just be alright to call and find out if he made it home safely? Would he think I was being goofy to call for that? Thoughts kept racing through my mind and I couldn't quite simmer down. Mom always told me that I could talk to God about anything. Well, tonight was going to be the night that I would have a long talk with God. Something had to give because I was not liking the way that I was feeling. I got my bible out and thought to myself, where do I start? I just simply opened my mouth and said, "Lord, I need your help, I don't know what to do and if you are really real and answer prayers like my mother is always saying that you do, you need to help me tonight." I opened my bible and it landed on Proverbs

3: 5,6. My mother is always highlighting certain scriptures and this one loomed out at me.

Trust in the Lord with all of thine heart; and lean not unto thine own understanding. In all thy ways acknowledge him, and he shall direct thy paths. (KJV)

Well, I needed God to do something for me this evening because I was not feeling like I knew how to handle what was going on in my mind and in my heart.

"I do trust you Lord, help me to understand what is going on and how to get a hold of myself."

I started to feel numb. Then like a soft wind of flurry, I felt a gentle wind of peace envelope me. It was as though God himself had come down and was rocking me in his arms. I begin to feel more steady and the song that we sang at choir rehearsal, (*What a friend we have in Jesus*) came to my mind as the promises of God in the words sang became so real to my spirit. Yes, God loved me so much that he would take the time to comfort a heart that felt broken and unsure. Why would God do that just for me? Well, he did, that night just for me. I got in bed and slept like a baby.

I almost woke up late but mom being such a on time person, banged on the door and reminded me that this is a school day and it was time to get up.

"How was school choir last night? Did you enjoy singing the songs?"

"It was good mom. Had a good time."

The pit of my stomach churned and I remembered last night. How am I going to get through this day without feeling so abandoned as I did last night? What am I going to do when I see Steve? Sure, just act like nothing is wrong. But Steve and I are friends and I always tell him how I feel, especially since our parents were going through the same things in their marriage. But could I share this with him and our relationship remain the same? Would he feel like he was obligated to like me just because I liked him. What if he did like Gloria, what would I do? Would I be able to handle it and wish him well. Would I be able and willing to allow him to form a new friendship with Gloria? Or would I fight for him? Oh Lord, what is going on, I thought these things in my mind were gone. I can't stand these thoughts racing through my mind.

"Kimmy, are you alright? You seem so preoccupied. Do you have a test in school today? What's going on?

"Oh, mom, nothing's wrong. Is this Bible Study night? Do I have to go tonight? I don't feel that well. Could I just miss tonight?"

"Well Kimmy, you felt well enough to go to school choir last night, I am sure that by this evening you will be feeling better. So, 6:30 be ready."

"Ok, mom."

I saw Steve and Gloria come down the hallway and I didn't like it. I was fuming and didn't even say good morning when Steve caught up with me and said hi. He looked at me very strange and didn't know what to make of it. Gloria looked at me too but she knew exactly how I was feeling. She just smiled and turned away quickly. Steve tried to catch up with me as I ran to my second period.

"What is wrong with you Kimmy? What did I do? Are you alright?"

"I am so sorry, Steve, I have a lot on my mind. I didn't mean to tune you out like that."

"Kimmy, you know you can talk to me. What's up? Is your mom and dad fighting? You know we have always been there for each other. Talk to me."

Part of me wanted to say, yes, I am being jealously mad at you because you seemed so happy walking with Gloria and she seemed so happy walking with you that I just felt like a third wheel. Somehow, I couldn't say that to Steve because he probably wouldn't understand my feelings. I didn't understand it either so how could I expect him to understand what I was going through.

"Steve, thanks so much, but I'll be alright. No, my mother and father are not fighting. I will see you at lunch time, gotta go."

"OK, by the way, Gloria wants to join us for lunch and I said it would be OK. I know you two will become real good friends. We had such a good time last night at school choir."

I just looked at him as he ran for his second period class. How could he do this to me? This was our time, and now he wants to include someone else. The remainder of the day was just a blur. When I arrived home at 4:30pm I was not in the mood to be haggled by Linda or Sissy. I just wanted to be left alone. My heart was hurting and I didn't know how to handle this battle that was before me.

"God, where are you when I need you?"

Mom called to us and said it was time to leave for bible study. Although I usually liked bible study, I was just not ready to hear anything this evening. I was hurting and I just wanted to be left alone. Mrs. Gray was teaching this evening and although she was not our regular teacher, my interest did perk up when she stated that the Lord dropped it in her spirit to talk about the battlefield of the mind. I couldn't believe my ears. She spoke of how the devil uses our minds to be tossed back and forth and to maneuver us into imagining things that would hinder us from being in control of our thoughts. Tears welled up in my eyes because I knew she was talking directly to me. God was letting me know that through his word, he could help me overcome those things that were besetting me. I didn't have to let those things control the way I think. I could have control through his word. I wrote down all of the scriptures that she quoted to me. I left bible study knowing that the battle was not mine but the Lords. I also realized that I could …."cast down all imaginations……." by using the word. God loved me so much that he did this just for me. I felt so special because I needed God and he came through for me. Just for me. In bed that night I felt that there was nothing I couldn't do because I had God on my side and I was going to implement what I had been taught. The devil was not going to do me like this again.

I got ready for school the next day and I was feeling pretty good. I saw Steve come down the hallway alone this time and I smiled at him and told him about the good time I had at bible study that evening. He remarked that he didn't make it to bible study last night because he was helping Gloria with her math homework. He said that she was having so much trouble and needed a tutor. My heart unexpectedly did a flip. How could this be happening. I thought my troubles were over. I tried to steady myself and not come unglued.

"Kimmy, what is wrong? You really have been looking and acting kind of strange lately."

"Steve, I will be fine, just need to sit down. Think I ate something that didn't agree with my stomach. I'll be alright."

"You seem to really be out of sorts lately, maybe you need to have a check up or something. I am really getting concerned. You are my friend Kimmy and I don't want anything to happen to you. Is there anything you need me to do? I just want to help."

"Oh, Steve, you are so sweet. I don't know what I would do if we couldn't be friends. Thanks for caring."

"Well, that's what friends are for. I do want to share something with you though. Gloria and I are going to the movies this weekend. I didn't realize that she wants to be friends with me as in boyfriend, girlfriend. She ask me if we were boyfriend and girlfriend. I told her that we were the best of friends but didn't have that kind of relationship and that you were like a little sister to me and the best friend a guy could have. This is my first friendship with a girl and I want things to be right Kimmy. What do you think?"

I couldn't believe what he was saying to me. My head went into a spend and I could only focus for a second before I burst out crying.

"Kimmy, you must really be sick. I am going to call your mom and tell Mr. Stone that you may need to go home."

"No, please don't do that. I will be alright. Just please leave me alone. I can't talk right now. Please Steve, just leave me alone. I will be alright."

I didn't have lunch with Steve that day and resigned myself to not see him again. My heart couldn't take it. I wrote Steve a letter and told him that I thought that he should concentrate on being friends with Gloria because I didn't want her to feel like I was imposing on her time with him. He said he understood but I think he was kind of glad because he really liked Gloria and enjoyed spending time with her in a boyfriend girlfriend relationship. Several months went by and even though I had first period with Gloria and Steve, I kept focusing on God's word about the battle belonging to him and that my mind was subject to the promises of God to be able to cast out all fear, doubt and anger. Each night and morning that I read the word of God and spoke the promises of God into my life, my days began to take on a new step toward recovery. It was so hard at first but I was determined that God did not intend for me to keep hurting like this and I had to believe his word. Then lighting struck again. Steve called me and stated that he needed to talk to me. I was surprised but kind of curious as to what he wanted to talk to me about. Perhaps he began to see the light. Maybe now he knows what a fool mistake he made and he wants to profess his undying love to me. I smiled to myself and said sure.

"Where do you want to meet?"

"Kimmy, lets talk at your house in your backyard. Do you think your mom would mind?"

"Of course not Steve, my mom likes you and thinks you are a pretty good guy. Come on over. I made the best oatmeal cookies, your favorite to be exact."

"Ok, be there in five."

I was so excited that I couldn't keep from smiling ear to ear. The long awaited time had come and now we were going to finally be together. Just me and Steve. He was going to see that I am the only girl for him.

"Hey, Kimmy, I have really missed talking with you. You are my best friend and I guess since I started going with Gloria we haven't spent much time together at all. Oh, I really miss you, can we talk?"

"Sure come on in, my mom is resting so we can go outside and talk in the backyard."

My heart was beating so fast and I just couldn't keep the smile I had on my face from beaming from ear to ear. I wondered if he could hear my heart and know how deeply I felt. I just wanted to fall into his arms and declare my undying love for him. Steve sat real quiet and didn't say anything at first.

"Steve, are you alright? Talk to me. I am your friend. I really care about how you are feeling."

"Kimmy, I have gotten myself into a real mess. Gloria is pregnant. I just can't believe that I let myself get out of control and this happened. We talked about God being first in our lives and that we didn't want to become intimate until things were right in our relationship. I really enjoyed being in her company but she always wanted to kiss and touch me in ways that made my mind go crazy. I just wanted to have a relationship with her like I had with you. I wanted us to be able to laugh and talk and be free of problems that hurt relationships. We talked about these things Kimmy. What happened?"

Before I could answer Steve, I had to get myself together. I am 16 now and since talking to Steve on the level that we use to talk, I had begun to look at things a little differently. I had to change course because I had gotten myself ready for a profession of love from Steve that was not there. I had to become the friend that he was used to talking to. Although he was 17 now and almost ready to graduate from high school, I had to be the friend that he wanted to lean on now. I was so shocked that I almost couldn't get my words together. Steve and Gloria, becoming parents together and forever blocking my life with Steve. Oh boy, I really had to regroup.

"Steve, I don't know what to say. I am just so surprised. Have you told anyone other than me? What is Gloria going to do? Both of you are just about to graduate from high school. Wow, I can't believe this."

"Gloria doesn't want to have the baby. She wants to have an abortion. She said that she is not ready to be a mother. She knows that it is wrong but she said that her mother agrees and that she is going to have it done this weekend. I have such mixed emotions. I know that I am not ready to be a father yet either, but just the thought of that tiny baby inside of Gloria being a part of me, I just can't get that out of my mind. I would rather she give the baby up for adoption so that one day we could see him or her again. But she doesn't want to do that. She won't even talk to me. I have made such a mess of things and have let God down. How could I have done this. I just wanted things to be right between us."

So many things were going through my mind. Now he wants to talk to me because he is in trouble. He doesn't love me, he just wants to use me to ease the pain that he is going through now. But my mind was also saying that this is what friends are for, to talk to when your comfort zone has been disrupted. I stood there in silence as Steve continued to pour out his heart to me. I listened and begin to hear the Holy Spirit talk to my spirit and touch it in a way that was so profound and loving that I had to smile at God. OK, you win, Lord. Steve is my friend and I am going to comfort him with your word.

"Steve, God loves you. At such a time as this, He has prepared so many promises to ease your pain and to give you direction. He just wants you to trust in him and know that he has your best interest in mind. We make mistakes but God is faithful that he will forgive you and cleanse you unto all unrighteousness. Trust Him Steve. Lets pray.

"Father, I bring Steve to you today. I lift his struggles and trials before you knowing that you are a loving God that forgives us of all our sins and brings us back into right standing with you. Touch my dear friend Lord and help him to understand that he can depend on you to make his way right. In Jesus' name I pray. Amen."

"Steve, things may be a little bumpy for you in your relationship with Gloria right now but trust God to bring you out of this a better person."

"Kimmy, thank you for praying for me. Please don't ever stop being my friend. I am not sure what I would have done if I didn't have you to talk to at this time. I will talk with you tomorrow."

"Goodnight Steve, talk to you soon."

As the door closed behind Steve I knew that our friendship was a good one but that we both still had a lot to learn. I could not be what he wanted me to be at this time. God was becoming so real to me in ways that I couldn't fathom. Was I becoming my mother, looking to God for everything? Was God becoming the center of my life? Yes, God heard my prayer for Steve and answered again a prayer for me........

SIX

The Fiat

The noise in my little fiat was so loud that I was ashamed to drive down the street. Thank goodness Dave would be home this weekend so hopefully he could find out what the problem was or get it fixed. It seemed like every time I turned around something was wrong in the house or with the car. Only two more blocks and I will be at work. Car pooling was good but I was too ashamed to let anyone ride in my car at this time. I had been carpooling for six months now and it really help save on gas since I was now driving almost 80 miles round trip everyday.

My co-worker, Shirley, was pulling up with her husband and waved hello to me.

"Oh, hi Shirley, how are ya?"

"Hi there Megan, good to see you. Hey, my husband needs to use the car today, do you think I could get a ride home with you after work? Tried calling before I left but you were already gone."

"No problem Shirley, that's if you don't mind hearing rumbling in my car. I am not sure what is wrong but Dave will be home this weekend and I really hope he can fix the car."

"No, I need a ride and we will just chuck along together", laughed Shirley.

It was 5:00pm and time to depart. Walking to the car dreading that noise was a bummer. As I waited on Shirley, I thought to myself,

Lord, I am so tired of handling all of these problems one right after another. It seemed liked once I got one fire out another one would ignite. What was going on? Don't people have lives that just sail around in nothing being wrong sometime? Lord, do I have a brand on my head?

"Thanks again Megan for letting me ride with you. My hubby had an important interview today and he needed the car. So glad I have a friend that I can depend on in a bind."

"Are you coming to church tonight? You know we have a special guest speaker and he is going to be teaching on Prayer. I really want to hear what he has to say because so many people don't really know how to hear from God and what to do when certain prayers are not being answered."

"Yea, it sounds like a topic I really want to hear discussed too. Why don't I pick you up after dinner and we can ride together to church."

"Sounds good, thanks Megan, you are such a wonderful friend."

Dave arrived home before I did and heard that loud noise and wondered what on earth was wrong.

"Dave, the car has been sounding like this for three days and I don't know what is wrong. I stopped at the gas station and the mechanic looked at it but said he would have to do a diagnostic on it to determine exactly what the problem is so I just chose to wait until you got home."

"Not sure if I know what's wrong either. I'll call Greg and see if he can come by to take a look at it. I have a lot of work to do this weekend that needs to be completed before I return to work on Monday so I am going to be real busy."

I wasn't surprised to hear him say this. Work always came first no matter what was going on. I looked at my watch and I had one hour before leaving for church. So glad Dave started dinner. The girls always liked when he cooked. Dave always cooked to perfection. If he cooked lamb, it was the best leg of lamb. Even if it was just chicken, it looked like it could be on the front page of a cooking magazine. I must say that I really enjoyed Dave's cooking for us because he always seemed to do his best to make it a special occasion. The girls wanted to stay home with Dave this evening so I didn't argue with them about coming to church with me. They really needed time to spend with him while he was at home so I didn't put up a fuss. I put the last minute touches on my make-up before leaving to pick up Shirley. When we arrived at the church we were amazed to see so many cars parked in the parking lot. Wow, so many people were out tonight to hear this special speaker. As we entered the church I couldn't believe that there were hardly any seats left. I always liked being near the front so that I could see good and hear the speaker without having to listen to people talk while the speaker was teaching.

"Shirley, I can't believe how many people are out tonight. Who is this speaker? Have you ever heard of him?"

"I don't know who he is Megan but I see him standing near the pastor. He's that light-skinned man, seems like he might be 6"2' around maybe 64 or 65 yrs old. Kinda hard to say. Never seen him before but he must be pretty good for all of these people to be here tonight. I even see people that don't go to this church".

Service was about to start and everyone was seated. Our pastor introduced the man of God to the congregation and everyone went into an uproar just clapping and responding to him standing. I thought to myself, wow, this man must be really important and have a word to say tonight. I had heard so many teachings and preachings on prayer that it didn't phase me at all that he was going to teach on this topic. He began to speak and THEN he began to TEACH. My attention now was on every word he was saying because something started to resonate in my spirit and I hungered to hear more of what he was saying. I was listening to things that I had not heard before or rather didn't put much importance on as far as using God's word. He gave us scripture after scripture and I was writing so fast that I was afraid that I wasn't going to get down everything he said. My mind became alive and wanting to hear more of what this man of

God was saying. He was speaking to the very core of my spirit. I wrote down every step he gave us reflecting on the promises and prayers of petition to God. He said that we must SPEAK the word and stand firm on the promises of God without wavering. He said faith comes by hearing and hearing by the word of God. I had heard that before but it just seemed to envelope my spirit differently this night. He said that we must speak to our circumstances and if we are in position and right standing with God, our prayers are answered if we waiver not for God does not lie. He stressed the importance of prayer on a daily basis along with meditating and reading the word of God daily and not just when we find ourselves in trouble and then we want to run to God and ask for his help. He said we must have a personal relationship with God and broke it down where we could understand how and what it means to have a personal relationship with the almighty God. I was so excited to hear this man of God and knew that he was definitely sent by God. When I found out he would have tapes for us to purchase my heart was made glad for I didn't want to miss out on anything that I may have forgotten to write down. Shirley and I left church that evening with an excitement in our footsteps that was overwhelming. What a mighty God we serve.

Shirley asked me if she could ride with me to work the next day and if Godzilla had asked I would have said yes. I woke up the next morning with such a zeal in my step that I felt I could do anything. Shirley was feeling the same way and we had so much to talk about on the way to work that I almost forgot about the noise in the car. My car was still clanking loudly and I wondered if Dave had called the guy to look at the car. Dave told me that I probably would have to drive like this for another week because Greg told him that it sounded like it was going to cost quite a bit to fix this problem. Then all of a sudden, I thought to myself. I believe God's word. I wrote down many of the promises that the man of God was telling us about. And because I knew that God does supply all of my needs, why wasn't I standing on the promise of him supplying my need and speaking to the circumstance knowing that God hears my prayer and will answer. I took a step with a leap of faith to believe on the word of God. I stood firm by speaking the word that he gave me. My friend Shirley stood with me placing her faith with mine. We prayed and got into the car and I drove to work. The clanking seemed like it got louder but even in the midst of the clanking and rumbling we kept praising God for his goodness and his mercy and supplying what I needed. When we arrived at work, people were looking at us because the car was making such a awful noise. Sure, I was embarrassed but I didn't utter a word. The word had already gone out and because I believed that his word would not return null or void I was praising Him for answered prayer.

We had a full day of work ahead and I didn't even think about the car until I got in to start it that evening. I pulled out of the driveway and I didn't hear anything. I looked at Shirley and she looked at me. We didn't say anything to each other for about ten minutes and as we were driving, tears welled up in my eyes and I thought about the goodness of our amazing God. "He fixed my car Shirley, Oh, he fixed my car", I shouted out as my voice began to crack. We both began to praise God and cried so much I didn't think we would be able to make it home. I kept waiting to hear the sound again but no sound came. Again, God showed up in a most astounding way. His word manifested as I stood in position and spoke to my circumstances believing that is word would do what he said it would do.

My walk with God began an even greater course. I had heard a man of God who yielded to the most High God and delivered a message to me that changed the very essence of my understanding and my love for God. I had always thought that I didn't have the ability to grasp profound messages that I thought only the elite had privy to. But God is no respecter of person and if we allow ourselves to learn of Him, speak the word as we believe on His word, love Him with all of our hearts, we can reap the benefits and promises that Jesus died for....... and again God answered prayer in a most astounding way. He used a vessel to speak to another vessel who heard His word and acted on it.

SEVEN

The Tithe

A letter came in the mail showing that we were two months behind in our mortgage. I didn't know what we were going to do because I didn't like asking anybody for money especially since I didn't know when we could pay them back. Dave was doing the best that he could but it seemed like more money was going out than was coming in. I have always been a tither and a believer in God's word. Kimmy ask me one Sunday, "why are you still putting money in church when we don't have very much?" She knew that our circumstances had changed and she couldn't understand the logic. But I have always believed that God's word is what it is. God says,

Bring ye all the tithes into the storehouse, that there may be meat in mine house, prove me now herewith, saith the Lord of hosts, if I will not open you the windows of heaven, and pour you out a blessing, that there shall not be room enough to receive it. (Malachi 3:10 KJV)

I have experienced so many blessings from the Lord, and in my thinking, I wasn't sure how he was going to do certain things, I just trusted and knew that he would.

My brother-in-law called that evening to find out how we were doing. We hadn't talked with him for awhile so I was really surprised to hear from him. He knew things were kind of tight for us but didn't know that we were in default with the mortgage. He kept asking me how we were really doing and I didn't want to tell him the real truth. I sort of stammered my way through the answers and then he just ask me point blank if we were behind in any bills. I told him our house payment was in default but we would be alright. He said, "I am going to send you $10,000 so that you guys can get on your feet."

"What, are you serious? We can't pay the money back right away?

"Just take care of my nieces."

My hands were shaking as God used my brother-in-law as a means to supply what we needed. He touched a heart that would be obedient to his moving and blessed us through an open door from heaven. How could we not serve and love a God who cares and does so much for His people.

EIGHT

The Shoes

I was looking in the mirror one morning and wondered to myself, God, I wonder what it would be like to have hardly any moles on my face. You see, I had quite a few moles and although it looked cute sometimes, I didn't really like looking at them on my face. So I was going to make my yearly appointment to have the moles checked when the phone rang. I had just finished praying with Shirley and found out that choir rehearsal would be canceled this evening. I was kind of glad because work was exceptionally busy this week and I was really tired. My feet hurt so badly I just wanted to rest. I was looking through some shoe magazines when I came across some flats that caught my eye. They looked alright but the fact that they came in a D width also caught my eye. A blue pair and a black pair were being shown and I said to myself I sure wish I could have those shoes right now because I didn't think I could take another day standing so much and not having comfortable shoes on my feet. I knew we needed so many other things and the fact that Dave's job was downsizing was in the back of my mind also. I needed to go by the hospital to see one of the members of the church, bake a cake for Molly, Kimmy's friend, who has a birthday coming soon and go over the notes for deaconess meeting which was tomorrow night. I felt that I had so much on my plate but I enjoyed doing things for the Lord. He had blessed me so much, the least that I can do is be a vessel to be used by him. When I think of all that the Lord has done for me my heart is so overjoyed. I just wanted my ways to please Him. I have learned that the best way to please God is to have a lifestyle of obedience that glorifies and honors His name.

I checked my mailbox and found that I had a package. I didn't remember ordering anything so to my surprise I opened the package and there in the box were two pairs of shoes. I couldn't believe my eyes. The shoes that I had seen in the shoe magazine were in the boxes. A blue pair and a black pair and the size was 8 1/2 D width. My size. I thought to myself, I only talked to God about these shoes. How could anyone else know about this. I called Dave and asked him if he had ordered some shoes for me and he said no. I called my sister-in-law and she didn't know anything about ordering any shoes either. I talked to several other people that I thought would do something like this and no one knew what I was talking about. I called the place where the shoes came from because I was beginning to think that maybe someone was playing a joke on me. They stated that the shoes were paid for but they were not at liberty to state who paid for them or give me any information about payment. I couldn't believe what was before my eyes. Two pairs of shoes that I had a conversation with God about appears in my mailbox. This was unbelievable. I knew that someone had to be playing a trick on me. I even talked to my co-workers and they looked at me like I was kind of loose in the head. Someone had ordered some shoes with my exact size and color, paid for them and they were delivered to ME at my address. How could this be.....

A couple of months passed and no one called stating that a mistake had been made or that I had to send the shoes back. I recalled my prayer to the Lord and it didn't seem any different than any other prayer that I would have prayed. I talked and communicated with God always knowing that he hears my prayers and answers. I was dumbfounded in the way that he did it but wore my shoes proudly. I continued to wonder for a while and thought the company was going to tell me that they delivered the shoes to the wrong person. It never happened and I am proud to know that God did an amazing wonder for me to let me know that I am not alone and that he can always be depended upon. I told so many people about what God did for me and that he is no respecter of persons. The same thing that he did for me he will do for anyone who lives a life devoted to his word, living his word and developing a relationship with a God who wants to do abundantly more than we can ever think or imagine. What an amazing and mighty God we serve !!!!!!

NINE

The Moles

"Hello, this is Megan Strauss, I would like to make an appointment to have the moles on my face checked. Yes, 3:00 o'clock Wednesday afternoon is fine. OK, I will see you then".

"Megan, I thought you had those moles checked a few months ago. Why are you having them checked again so soon. Is everything alright?"

"Dave, I had a regular check up a few months ago and forgot to have the moles checked at the same time. One of the moles seems to be getting larger and it sort of itches a little so I just want to make sure everything is alright. How are things going at the job?"

"Pretty good for me, but there is so much tension in the air. I am not sure what to do at times Megan, can you and your bible friends pray that some of the other workers don't get laid off?

"You know I will pray for the other workers Dave. God knows their needs and wants the best for them. OK, don't look at me like that, I am not going to start preaching at you. I just wanted to remind you of how much God cares."

Dave always feels like I am preaching at him when I tell him about the word of God. I just want him to realize that he can depend on God for any and everything. I waited for Dave to leave the room and I began to talk to God in the solitude of my kitchen. Although my bedroom is the main place I surrender my all to the Lord, I didn't want to wait until bedtime or try to hide in the bathroom while Dave was in our room watching TV. I pondered over the things that had happened that day and regrouped with God. "Dave is very concerned about the lay offs at his job. Lord, I thank you for favor at Dave's workplace that no workers will suffer layoff. I know Dave acts ungrateful at times but he does have a good heart and he does know that you are real. And Lord, one more thing. I thank you that when I go to have my moles checked that all will be well with the moles. These things I pray, in Jesus name. Amen."

"Hey, Kimmy, how was your day at school? Where is Laura?"

"She's coming, walks so slow sometimes.....did you finish baking the cake for Molly? We are going to surprise her in class tomorrow. Oh, mom, you didn't forget did you? I promised everyone that I would bring the cake."

"The cake is right there on the counter. Surprise you didn't see it when you came in the door. And thank you? I took off from work today to get some things done and that project is completed. I hope she likes it. You did say a strawberry cake, didn't you?"

"Yes, that's her favorite, she is going to be so surprised. Ever since her mother passed away we have been trying as her classmates to make her feel better so she won't miss her mom so much. I just don't know what I would do if you or dad left us. Oh, mom, it makes me feel so scared to even think of not having both of you taking care of us."

"Sweetheart, don't fret, we are here for you. And always remember that God loves you best and he will always take care of you in so many ways. That's why I want you and Laura to know about the Lord and learn to talk to Him and depend on Him for everything. Is Molly going to stay here with her aunt or is she going to Boston to live with her dad?"

"I don't know yet. I don't even think she has made her mind up yet. She has never really spent a lot of time with her father but he wants her to transfer to Boston to finish school there. He seemed so hurt when she said that she wanted time to think about coming to live with him. She has all summer to think about it now that school is almost out. I sure hope she decides to stay. I will miss her so much if she leaves. She is my best friend."

"Well, let's just pray that she makes the wisest decision. Her father seems to really care about her and she needs to get to know him better. She might be surprised how good it feels to be with a parent especially if one is already gone home to be with the Lord."

"Mom, Molly's father is not a Christian. And that is one of the reasons she doesn't want to go live with him."

"Well, she is old enough to say she wants to go to church. That doesn't have to be a reason not to be with your family. Your dad is not a Christian. Would that be a reason for you to not want to be with him?"

"Of course not mom. Dad lives here already but Molly doesn't really even know her father that well. I feel so bad for her. Sometimes she just sits and cries and misses her mom so much."

"We will have to have her over for dinner some evening and pray with her, OK?"

"OK."

Wednesday is here and time to head out for the appointment to have moles checked. Oh no, did I tell Shirley that I had to leave work early for my appointment. It seems like I am always forgetting things. I just hope she has another way to get home.

"Shirley, I have to leave work early, forgot to mention that I have a doctor's appointment today at 3:00 o'clock. Will you be able to get another ride home?"

"Not a problem, Megan. Jessie goes my way, so I will ask her for a ride. She is always telling me that I can have a ride any time. I will give her a call. This will even maybe give me an opportunity to witness to her." (thumbs up) It's 2:50 pm and I have time to use the restroom before my appointment. I have been holding it since I left work. I keep telling myself I need to go when I first feel it instead of waiting to the very last minute. But some habits are so hard to break. I guess when I have an accident then I will definitely break the habit.

There were five people in the doctor's office and I am wondering to myself if I am going to have to wait a long time before seeing the doctor. Could be a time to just relax and read a book. Before I could think about how long or what if, the receptionist calls my name. Wow, I got here just in time.

"Hello, Mrs. Strauss, please have a seat. The doctor will be in shortly."

As I sat in the room waiting for the doctor I started reading all of these books about the different kinds of moles and what changes to look for and when to become concerned about those changes. I kept thinking to myself, did this mole look the same way that it did last year, did it itch a long time or just for a short while. Should I really be concerned and say something to him about it or should I just wait and see if continues to itch or change in another way. Wow, decisions, decisions. The doctor comes in and introduces himself.

"Good afternoon, Mrs. Strauss, I am Dr. Lisbon. How are you this afternoon?"

"I am fine, Dr. Lisbon. It's nice to meet you. Just here to have my moles checked. I try to do this every year since I have so many on my face."

"Yes, I see. (examining moles) You know these moles typically are not prone to be cancerous. I see that you mentioned that a couple of them have grown larger and one started to itch a little. Well, you really don't have anything to worry about. You know what I am going to do for you today. I am going to remove all of the moles on your face. I just feel like I want to bless you today."

I didn't know what to say or what to do. He explained that it would be a little painful when burning the moles off and that it would look scarred at first but in a few days the moles would fall off and my face would begin to heal. I couldn't believe what he was saying. Tears were rolling down my cheeks from the pain of the burning mixed with a happiness of something miraculous happening. I had talked to God and He was answering my prayer using this doctor. I kept asking myself, is this really happening to me? Did God care that much about even the moles on my face? Why would he do this for me? What did I do to deserve this blessing? After the procedure was completed, the doctor told me that this is a $3,000 procedure and to not mention this to anyone. How could I not tell anyone about a blessing that God had done especially for me? How could I not tell someone about the goodness and blessings of God. I shared my testimony with many people not saying who the doctor was or where he was located. I learned since then that this doctor was a minister and was definitely led by God to bless me that day. What a mighty God we serve!!!!! I have found that when you position yourself to be blessed with a right to stand on the promises of God and speaking boldly the word of God, manifestations of God's glorious works will be revealed..........

I left the doctor's office with such an excitement that I could hardly drive home without having to stop and pinch myself to make sure this was real. I just kept thinking about what the Lord did for me. When I arrived home I didn't say anything to Dave and he hardly noticed that anything was different. It took all of my composure to not shout out about what God did for me that day. I could share with Shirley because I knew she would be excited for me and with me. I didn't share it with Kimmy that evening because she was on the phone for hours with Molly. When I saw Shirley the next day and told her about what happened she was amazed and excited.

"Wow, God is amazing Megan. Will you pray with me in agreement for a job for my husband? He has been so down lately because of so many interviews and no call backs yet. We really need a breakthrough."

"Yes I will Shirley, but remember that we serve an all knowing God and what we sometimes view as negative feedback can many times serve as God's amazing protection from what might seem like a block for us but a door that is closed for a future blessing. God knows your needs and because you and your husband are believers and standing in right position, I know he will work speedily."

"Thanks Megan, I am so glad that we are friends.

And again God showed up answering prayer out of nowhere. Shirley's husband received a call back from a very small but growing company. The CEO was retiring and wanted to find someone that had a passion for growing a small company and because the CEO had planned wisely he started Shirley's husband's salary at a price twice what he had been making. The company Shirley's husband really wanted had a million dollar lawsuit filed against them. God is an amazing God that not only sees the needs of his people and protects them but also relishes to give us our desires. His word says,

Trust in the Lord, and do good; so shall thou dwell in the land, and verily thou shall be fed.

Delight thyself also in the Lord; and he shall give thee the desires of thine heart.

Commit thy way unto Lord; trust also in him; and he shall bring it to pass. (Psalms 37: 3-5 KJV)

Yes, we serve an almighty God who is just waiting for an opportunity to show all just how much he loves us. His promises are true and his love is overwhelming. He wants no one to perish but to have an everlasting life. If you have never made Jesus Christ your Lord and personal Savior, He is calling to your heart today. He wants desperately to show you just how much He loves you and wants to give you the desires of your heart too.

Allow Jesus to come into your heart and life today by simply asking Him to come in and save you from your sins. Totally commit and surrender your life to him today. He is waiting and desiring to bless you with eternal salvation and a way of life answering your prayers again and again just as He has answered mine..........